GUIDE TO RAPID REVISION

THE ODYSSEY PRESS
The Bobbs-Merrill Company, Inc. Publishers
Indianapolis · New York

DANIEL D. PEARLMAN

PAULA R. PEARLMAN

GUIDE TO RAPID REVISION

THE ODYSSEY PRESS

A DIVISION OF THE BOBBS-MERRILL COMPANY, INC.

PRINTED IN THE UNITED STATES OF AMERICA

Library of Congress Catalog Card Number: 65-25583

ISBN-0-672-63044-3(pbk)

Eleventh Printing

A NOTE TO THE TEACHER

We have long felt that the process of revision, central in the development of writing skills, has not been accorded the full attention it merits among books published for courses in English composition. The composition handbooks are designed primarily for *class* study of the problems of writing in a sequential and topically organized manner. The student who turns to them, depending on their aid when revising a paper marginally annotated by his teacher, finds that he loses time hunting for the passages relevant to his particular problem, and that he must often read as much as a full chapter for each error he has committed.

The present *Guide*, planned entirely with the realities of revision in mind, provides the student with *immediate* answers to the specific problems he encounters, gives him *all* the information he needs, and yet does so with *brevity*. Using the book independently, the student may feel as if the teacher were personally going over his paper with him point by point in conference.

The compactness of this *Guide*, and the alphabetical arrangement of its contents, are only two of its features. Another, which should add greatly to its utility, is its *Table of Correction Symbols*, a gathering of all the most common symbols used by English teachers throughout the country. A student referring to this table can revise his paper with no uncertainty as to his teacher's system of notation. We call attention also to the realistic examples, culled from actual student papers, that illustrate the various types of errors. In the brief explanations which in most cases follow each error, the general rule for correction is embodied in a living context.

Since the *Guide* is designed for independent use by the student, it becomes feasible for the teacher to have his students spend a period now and then revising their papers in class under his direct supervision. The clear, compact treatment of each topic in this *Guide* will enable the student to master a considerable number of his errors in short order; and the demands levied upon the teacher for individual help will be reduced to a workable minimum. You may find, also, that if each student is required to maintain the *Progress Charts* included at the end of this *Guide,* you will be able to diagnose at a glance, during conferences, the student's overall writing problems.

In brief, we feel that our *Guide to Rapid Revision* will be found valuable both in courses where a regular handbook of composition is assigned and in those, also, where no handbook is used. If necessary, the *Guide* can serve as a substitute for a handbook because it contains an adequate treatment, in spite of its small physical compass, of the basics of English style, usage, grammar, and mechanics.

A NOTE TO THE STUDENT

This book is designed to save you many hours in revising your compositions. Our aim has been to make explanations brief, clear, and to the point, and to include realistic examples that you can apply to correcting any specific error of your own. Years of teaching experience have convinced us that even your most serious writing problems can be done away with in short order. To attain our aim of brevity, however, we have sacrificed no information that could cast real light on your writing difficulties. At the same time that you correct your errors, you learn the principles of English usage involved, so that you need not repeat the same errors in the future.

How to use this Guide: If your instructor uses correction symbols, and you are not certain of their meaning, the *Table of Correction Symbols* will help you past this first obstacle to revision. The most commonly used symbols—for example, **frag** or **RO**—are listed in alphabetical order in the *Table*, each symbol followed by its meaning spelled out in full. A few nonalphabetical symbols, such as // and ¶, are listed at the end.

If you know the meaning of a particular symbol—for example, that **CS** means COMMA SPLICE—look up the word or words in the *Table of Contents* to find the page on which it is discussed. As you will note, the *Guide* is arranged in alphabetical order for your convenience. It is assumed throughout that you know the meanings of such basic grammatical terms as *noun, verb,* and *sentence;* hence, this book is not intended as a substitute for the usual manual of elementary grammar. In any case, the examples showing you how to correct each error will usually be of more direct help than any amount of abstract explanation could possibly be.

Special spelling problems are handled in the sections on ABBREVIATIONS and NUMBERS. We take it for granted that in the usual case of a misspelled word you will refer to your dictionary. If, in addition, you keep up to date your general *Progress Chart* and your *Spelling Progress Chart*—included at the end of the *Guide*—you will have an excellent understanding of your writing problems and what to bear down on as the term progresses.

All in all, we trust you will find this *Guide* to be the remedy you need to clear up all your revision headaches.

D. D. P.
P. R. P.

CONTENTS

CORRECTION SYMBOLS

ab	ABBREVIATION
abst	ABSTRACT EXPRESSION
adj	ADJECTIVE
adv	ADVERB
agr	AGREEMENT
amb	AMBIGUITY
ap, apos	APOSTROPHE (See Punctuation.)
awk	AWKWARDNESS
C	COMMA (See Punctuation.)
ca	CASE
cap	CAPITALIZATION
CF	COMMA FAULT (See Comma Splice.)
choppy	CHOPPY SENTENCES
coh	COHERENCE
comp	COMPARISON
CS	COMMA SPLICE
D	DICTION
dang	DANGLING MODIFIER
dict	DICTIONARY
DM	DANGLING MODIFIER
E, ex	EXACTNESS (See Diction.)
em, emph	EMPHASIS
fog	FOGGY WRITING
frag	FRAGMENTARY SENTENCE
inc	INCOMPLETE CONSTRUCTION
ital	ITALICS
K	AWKWARDNESS
mod	MISPLACED MODIFIER
mx	MIXED CONSTRUCTION
No cap	NO CAPITALIZATION
No ¶	NO PARAGRAPHING
No Pn	NO PUNCTUATION
num	NUMBERS
O	OMIT (See Wordiness.)

¶	PARAGRAPHING
P	PUNCTUATION
paral	PARALLELISM
pass	PASSIVE VOICE
PF	PERIOD FAULT (See Run-On Sentence.)
Pn	PUNCTUATION
PV	POINT OF VIEW (See Shift in Point of View.)
quot	QUOTATION MARKS (See Punctuation.)
R	REPETITION
ref	REFERENCE OF PRONOUN
rep	REPETITION
RO, RS, run-on	RUN-ON SENTENCE
semi	SEMICOLON (See Punctuation.)
shift	SHIFT IN POINT OF VIEW
sp	SPELLING (See Abbreviations and Numbers.)
SS	SENTENCE STRUCTURE
sub	SUBORDINATION
T	TENSE
tr	TRANSPOSE
trans	TRANSITION
trite	TRITENESS
U, un	UNITY (See Coherence.)
und	UNDERLINE (See Italics.)
Us	USAGE (See Diction.)
var	VARIETY IN SENTENCE PATTERNS
vb	VERB (See Tense.)
W, wd, WW	WRONG WORD (See Diction.)
wdy	WORDINESS
WO	WORD ORDER (See Transpose.)
//	PARALLELISM
¶	PARAGRAPHING
X	AN OBVIOUS ERROR
∧	INSERT WHAT WAS OMITTED

[ab] ABBREVIATIONS

As a general rule, do not use abbreviations in your writing. **Spell the word in full.**

Some of the most common ink-saving habits to get rid of are the following abbreviations: *&, gov't., U.S.* or *U.S.A.* USE: **and, government, United States, United States of America.**

A common "thought-saver" to avoid is *etc.,* short for *et cetera,* meaning *and so forth.* If the reader is not acquainted with everything you might mean by *etc.,* you can not expect him to read your mind and fill in the exact items you are thinking of.

Exceptions: With proper names, always use the abbreviated titles **Dr., Mr., Messrs., Mrs., Mmes., Jr., Sr.,** and **St.** (Saint).

Other standard abbreviations are **A.M., P.M., A.D., B.C.,** and those of certain well-known organizations and government agencies, such as FBI, NATO, TVA.

[abst]   ABSTRACT EXPRESSIONS

Change the *abstract* term to one that is *concrete*.

ABSTRACT TERMS:

Abstract words, like *Americanism, beauty, evil, progress*, have meanings that are somewhat different for every individual reader. Perhaps you are certain of what you mean by "progress" in a statement such as this: "America has made great progress in the last fifty years." But your reader does not know what you mean until you use a more *specific* expression such as "technological progress" or "moral progress."

To avoid vagueness, you would no doubt further have to explain an expression like "moral progress." Do you mean that the divorce rate has gone down? Do you mean that teen-agers are more "moral"?

The effect of further explaining yourself is to get more and more *specific* and *concrete* in the ideas you project. The more you get down to brass tacks, the smaller is the danger of your being misunderstood.

CONCRETE TERMS:

A word is truly *concrete* when it refers to an actual object whose nature people are generally agreed on. For example, we all know what *tree* stands for. However, when the tree you are writing about has a place of importance in your composition, it is better to use an even more specific concrete expression, like *elm, oak,* or whatever it might be. It is like zooming in for a close-up in movie-making.

[adj]   ADJECTIVE

Change the word indicated to an adjective.

Certain verbs, like *look, sound, smell, taste,* and *feel,* are usually followed by adjectives instead of adverbs. (Adjectives used in this way describe, or "modify," the subject and are called predicate adjectives.)

Examples:

> You look *good.* (Use *well* only if you mean that the person no longer looks *ill!*)
> The food tasted *delicious.*
> I feel *good.* (I feel *well* means I am no longer *ill.*)
> The music sounds *wonderful.*
> The flower smells *fragrant.*

[adv]   ADVERB

Change the adjective to an adverb (usually by adding *-ly*).

In careless or very informal kinds of speech one hears errors such as the following:

Error: She sang *beautiful.*
Correction: *beautifully.* She sang beautifully.

Error: He writes pretty *good.*
Correction: pretty *well,* or, more formal, rather *well.* He writes pretty well.

Error: I had a *real* good time.
Correction: Avoid expressions such as *real good, real nice,*

and use instead *rather good* or *very good.* **I had a very good time.**

1. **Make your verb agree in number with its subject.** If your verb is in the singular, change it to the plural, and vice-versa.

2. **Make your pronoun agree in number with its antecedent** (the word your pronoun refers to).

1. SUBJECT-VERB AGREEMENT.

In ordinary sentences you can easily see how the subjects and verbs agree in number, as in the following examples:

> *He speaks* well. (Singular subject, "he"; singular verb, "speaks.")
> *They speak* well. (Plural subject and plural verb.)

Your mistakes occur in sentences where you are not sure of what the true subject is, and where you do not know whether the subject is singular or plural.

a. Don't be fooled by words and phrases which come between your subject and verb. Find the *simple* subject (the subject stripped of all its modifying words and phrases). *The simple subject is never part of a prepositional phrase.* But prepositional phrases often follow your subject and confuse you, as in the following sentences:

Error: The solution to all our problems *are* staring us in the face.

Correction: *is.* (The subject is *solution,* not *problems,* because "to all our problems" is a prepositional phrase.) **The solution to all our problems is staring us in the face.**

Error: One of the things I have read about *are* the debts this country has.

Correction: *is.* (The simple subject is *one,* not *things,* and not *debts* either.) **One of the things I have read about is the debts this country has.**

b. In some cases, normal sentence order is reversed and the subject *follows* the verb.

Error: After the cheerleaders *come* the band.

Correction: *comes.* (The band *comes.*) **After the cheerleaders comes the band.**

Error: There *is* two dogs in the park.

Correction: *are.* **There are two dogs in the park.** (Be careful of sentences beginning with *there* followed by a verb. *There* is never the subject—except in this very sentence! The subject will always follow the verb. In this example, *two dogs* is a plural subject, and therefore takes a plural verb. But note this important exception: "There is a bottle of wine in the cupboard and a thick hunk of cheese." Although *bottle* and *hunk* form a double, or compound, subject, and should logically take a plural verb, *are,* we keep the more natural sounding *is.* The *idiom* of the language sometimes violates grammatical *logic.* As long as the *first part* of the compound subject in a "there is" sentence is singular, the verb may also remain in the singular: "There *is* one man against the proposal and five men in favor of it."

c. When singular subjects are joined by *either-or, neither-nor,* use a singular verb.

Error: Neither the captain nor the coach *have* much experience.

Correction: *has.* **Neither the captain nor the coach has much experience.**

If one of the subjects joined by *or* or *nor* is plural, then the verb agrees with the nearer subject.

Error: Neither the captain nor the coaches *has* much experience.

Correction: *have.* (The plural, *coaches,* is nearer to the verb.) **Neither the captain nor the coaches have much experience.**

Error: Neither the coaches nor the captain *have* much experience.

Correction: *has.* (The singular, *captain,* is nearer to the verb.) **Neither the coaches nor the captain has much experience.**

2. PRONOUN-ANTECEDENT AGREEMENT.

Example: *Bill* knows *he* is smart.

The pronoun *he* refers to *Bill. Bill* is the "antecedent," the word referred to by the pronoun *he.*

Example: Immediately after buying his *books,* he lost *them.*

The antecedent of *them* is *books.* Notice that in both these examples, the pronoun agrees in number with its antecedent: *he* is singular, as is *Bill; them* is plural, as is *books.*

You make most of your mistakes when you forget to use a singular pronoun to refer to words such as *each, one, every, everybody, everyone, anybody, anyone, nobody, no one, either, neither.*

Error: Everybody raised *their* hand.
Correction: *his.* **Everybody raised his hand.**

Error: We felt that each of the workers loved *their* job.
Correction: *his.* (The antecedent is *each,* not *workers.*) **Each of the workers loved his job.**

[amb] AMBIGUITY

Ambiguity means *double* meaning or else *vagueness* of meaning. **Make the ambiguous word clearly mean one thing only.**

Ambiguity: Bob asked Jack if Iris liked *him.*

Correction: Use direct quotation. If *him* stands for Jack, write: **"Does Iris like you?" Bob asked Jack.**

(See REFERENCE OF PRONOUNS and MISPLACED MODIFIERS for further discussions. If the ambiguity is a general *vagueness* of meaning, see ABSTRACT EXPRESSIONS.)

[awk] [K] AWKWARDNESS

The word, phrase, or passage marked is clumsy and should be entirely rewritten.

The cause of awkward writing is often *foggy thinking.* If you first concentrate and get a sharp picture of your idea in your mind, you will then be able to express it clearly and accurately on paper. Here is an example of awkward writing—caused, of course, by foggy thinking:

"Our present world is quite materialistic; it is a world in which money, success and education are thriving over the love of nature itself."

.For one thing, does it make sense to say that money is "thriving"? Indeed, this sentence is so awkward that a complete correction might have to run like this:

"In our present materialistic world, our love for nature can not thrive in the face of our greater craving for money, success, and the kind of 'education' that helps us attain these goals." (See also COHERENCE.)

[cap]   CAPITALIZATION

Capitalize the word or words indicated, or else make them begin with a small letter if you have incorrectly used capitals.

1. Capitalize proper names. These are the names of specific persons, places, things, races, institutions, organizations: **Joe Fox, the East River, Negro, Tilden High School,** the **United Nations.** (Note: the word *the* beginning names of organizations should not be capitalized: *the United Nations, the Police Athletic League.*)

2. Capitalize the first word of every sentence, including the first word of every quoted sentence:

   He said proudly, "Everything is in order."

3. For titles of books, articles, movies, and plays, always capitalize the first word and every word except small prepositions, conjunctions, and articles of four letters or less: **The Old Man and the Sea; Much Ado About Nothing; Life with Father.**

[ca]   CASE

Use the correct case of the pronoun (either the subjective case, the objective case, or the possessive case). For *nouns* in the possessive case look up how to use the apostrophe under PUNCTUATION.

A hint for speedy correction: Here is a list of the problem-pronouns in all their three cases. Pick out the pronoun you have misused and note what case it is in. Obviously the correct form must be one of the other two case-forms. Look up the examples of *errors* given for these other two case-forms, and you will find one similar to your own as well as the correct form you should use. Here are the six troublesome pronouns and their cases:

Subjective case:	I	we	he	she	they	who
Objective case:	me	us	him	her	them	whom
Possessive case:	my	our	his	her	their	whose

Note: If the error you have is *it* or *it's,* change the word to *its* (the correct spelling of the possessive case).

1. SUBJECTIVE CASE.

If the pronoun is gramatically the *subject* of the sentence or clause, then keep it in the *subjective* case.

Error: My brother and *me* double-date very often.

Correction: *I.* ("My brother and I" is the subject. Would you say, "*Me* double-date"?) **My brother and I double-date very often.**

Error: All three of them, John, Willy, and *him,* witnessed the accident.

Correction: *he.* ("John, Willy, and *he*" is in apposition to the subject of the sentence, *all.* You would not say, "*Him* witnessed the accident.") **All three of them, John, Willy, and he, witnessed the accident.**

Error: I am as tall as *him.*

Correction: *he.* (Think of the sentence in this way: I am as tall as he [is]. *He* is the subject of an understood verb, *is.*) **I am as tall as he.**

Error: We climbed faster than *them.*

Correction: *they.* (Here again, there is an understood verb: We climbed faster than they [did].) **We climbed faster than they.**

Error: I enjoy speaking to *whom*ever wants to learn mechanics.

Correction: *who*ever. (Remember that the object of the preposition *to* is not *whomever*, or even *whoever*, but the whole clause, "whoever wants to learn mechanics." *Who*ever is naturally the subject of this clause, and *wants* is the verb. *The case of the pronoun is decided solely by the pronoun's position inside its own clause.* Very simply, you wouldn't say, "*Whom* wants"; you would say, "*Who* wants.") **I enjoy speaking to whoever wants to learn mechanics.**

Error: He revealed *whom* he thought would win.

Correction: *who.* (The writer here may have been fooled by two things: 1. He may have thought that *whom* is the object of the verb *revealed.* The object, however, is the whole clause "who he thought would win." 2. The writer may have thought that *whom* was a direct object in its own clause. He was fooled by the words "he thought," which is a parenthetical expression that comes between the true subject-verb combination, *who would win.* See further examples in the following discussion of the objective case.) **He revealed who he thought would win.**

2. OBJECTIVE CASE.

If the pronoun is the object of a verb or of a preposition, then keep it in the *objective* case.

Error: The fire was put out by us, Jim and *I.*

Correction: *me.* (*Me,* just like *us,* is in the objective case after the preposition *by.*) **The fire was put out by us, Jim and me.**

Error: I was not sure *who* she liked.

Correction: *whom.* (Rearrange the sentence to see clearly the subject-verb-object pattern: She liked *whom. Whom* is object of the verb *liked.*) **I was not sure whom she liked.**

Error: Nobody knew *who* he was talking about.

Correction: *whom.* (In the whole clause, "whom he was talking about," *whom* is the object of the preposition *about.* Rearrange the clause to see the pattern clearly: **He was talking about *whom.*) Nobody knew whom he was talking about.**

3. POSSESSIVE CASE.

The use of the possessive pronoun before the gerund often gives students trouble.

Error: I did not approve of *him* going by himself.

Correction: *his.* (A pronoun that comes directly before a gerund—a verbal used as a noun—is ordinarily in the possessive case.) **I did not approve of his going by himself.**

[choppy] CHOPPY SENTENCES

Revise your series of short, choppy sentences by varying your sentence patterns. Do not simply combine your sentences with "and's" or semicolons. The result of that would be a series of *longer* choppy sentences. If you master the very simple art of using a variety of sentence types, your style will become much smoother and your grade will improve considerably. If you read the few simple examples under VARIETY IN SENTENCE PATTERNS, you can master the art of smooth and rhythmic sentences in short order.

[coh]   COHERENCE

Completely rewrite the indicated passage. As it now stands, the material does not make clear, logical sense on a first reading. The parts are not coherently organized to follow one another in a logical pattern.

Suggestion for revision: Clarify in your own mind the ideas you wanted to express. Then imagine yourself attempting to explain these ideas as clearly as possible to a friend who knows nothing of the subject, or to a younger brother or sister. If you put yourself fully into this dramatic situation, there is no doubt that you will clear up the lack of coherence in your writing.

A SAMPLE PARAGRAPH LACKING COHERENCE:

In "Song of Myself," Walt Whitman speaks of his feelings toward nature and life in all its aspects. He loves anything that is unlimited by conventions and expresses itself freely. He can only feel a liking toward limited things.

Love, for him, is the greatest form of awareness. "Never let anything put you into a rut" seems to be his motto.

The above paragraph is a typically incoherent piece of writing. Not only is there a lack of logical continuity from one sentence to another, but the fog and confusion is made murkier by phrasing, as in the third sentence ("He can only feel a liking," etc.), which says just the opposite of what the writer meant. In addition, this paragraph commits the typical error of omitting necessary steps in the logical sequence of ideas, so that one thought appears to have nothing to do with the next. (See also AWKWARDNESS.)

THE SAME PARAGRAPH MADE COHERENT—AND NECESSARILY LONGER:

In "Song of Myself," Walt Whitman speaks of his boundless love for nature, a concept which includes all things that exist. He loves especially anything or anyone who expresses his inmost drives freely and does not allow himself to be limited by deadening conventions. He acclaims the force of love in the universe as a whole, for love destroys all limiting conventions and leads us to freedom by giving us greater and greater awareness of ourselves and the world about us. Whitman can feel only sympathy, not love, for people limited by tradition and custom. He would prefer that we kept this motto in mind: "Never let anything put you into a rut." (Of course, it would now be better not to include the last sentence with its shabby "motto.")

COMMA SPLICE

Do not join, or "splice," two separate sentences with a comma. **Change the comma to a period (or to a semicolon,** if you are certain how to use it: see PUNCTUATION).

Error: New York is a busy industrial city, thousands of cars, trucks, and buses move through it every day.

Correction: Change the comma after *city* to a period and capitalize *thousands,* which is now the first word of a new sentence. You could also correct the error by changing the comma after *city* to a semicolon [;]. **New York is a busy industrial city. Thousands of cars, trucks, and busses move through it every day.** [*Or*] **New York is a busy industrial city; thousands of cars, trucks, and busses move through it every day.**

A second type of comma splice error is made in the case of sentences beginning with words such as *therefore, however, then, nevertheless, moreover, also, still, thus,* or with expressions such as *in fact, for example, that is, on the other hand, in other words.* These are transitional words or phrases which begin a new main clause or a new sentence. Most often the main clause beginning with such an expression should be linked with the previous main clause by a semicolon. Study the following examples:

Error: We packed all our luggage, then we were on our way to the airport.

Correction: Change the comma after *luggage* to a semicolon. **We packed all our luggage; then we were on our way to the airport.**

Error: He did not arrive in time, therefore we had no choice but to leave without him.

Correction: Place a semicolon after *time.* **He did not arrive in time; therefore we had no choice but to leave without him.**

Error: I have always loved sports, in fact, I was once the youngest member of my team in the Little League.

Correction: Place a semicolon after *sports.* **I have always loved sports; in fact, I was once the youngest member of my team in the Little League.**

[comp] | **COMPARISONS**

Your comparison is either incomplete or illogical. **Find your error and correct it by referring to the examples below.**

1. INCOMPLETE COMPARISONS.

Error: The world is excessively materialistic. We should be more concerned with our inner selves.

Correction: (If you use *more,* or some other comparative, you must complete the comparison you have begun by using a statement with *than.*) **The world is excessively materialistic. We should be more concerned with our inner *than with our outer* selves.**

Error: As the years went by, group singing became more popular.

Correction: As the years went by, group singing became more popular *than solo performances.*

Error: I like Jane because she is different.

Correction: (Do not use *different* as a synonym for *un-usual.* Complete the comparison begun with *different* by adding a logical statement beginning with *from.*) **I like Jane because she is different *from all the other girls I know.***

2. ILLOGICAL OR "FALSE" COMPARISONS.

Error: The traffic in New York City is worse than Chicago.

Correction: (In the error, *traffic* is illogically compared to a city!) **The traffic in New York City is worse than *the traffic in* Chicago.**

Error: In this poem, Robert Frost expresses ideas different from most other poets.

Correction: (In the error, *ideas* are illogically compared to *poets.*) **In this poem, Robert Frost expresses ideas different from *those of* most other poets.**

[dang] [DM]   DANGLING MODIFIERS

The modifier in your sentence "dangles" because it does not clearly and logically relate to another word in the sentence. **Rewrite the sentence** in either of two ways: 1) Change the dangling element into a subordinate clause by adding a subject and verb, or 2) Change the main clause so that the subject agrees with the dangling modifier.

Dangling modifiers appear in italics in the following examples:

Error: *When sitting*, my shoulders tend to slump back. ("I," the logical subject of the modifier, does not appear in the sentence. As now written, the sentence says "my shoulders" are sitting.)

Correction: 1. Change the dangling element into a subordinate clause: **When *I* sit, my shoulders tend to slump back.** 2. Change the subject of the main clause to agree with the dangling element: **When sitting, *I* find that my shoulders tend to slump back.**

Error: *To type well*, your legs must be in the correct position. (Are "your legs" doing the typing?)

Correction: 1. *If you want to type well*, your legs must be in the correct position. 2. To type well, *you must keep* your legs in the correct position.

Error: *Going home*, it started to drizzle. (Where is the subject who is "going"?)

Correction: 1. *As I was going home*, it started to drizzle. 2. Going home, *I felt it starting* to drizzle.

| **[D]** | **DICTION** |

Change the word you have used to one that is more exact in *meaning*, or to one that is more appropriate in *tone* to the rest of the composition.

Certain errors in diction recur so frequently that it might be worth your while to check your error against the *Glossary of Common Errors in Diction* that has been arranged alphabetically below. In any case, take the following two suggestions as a guide for correcting and avoiding mistakes in diction:

1. Check on the exact meaning of the word you have

used in a large (at least desk-sized) modern dictionary.

2. Check in your dictionary to see whether the word you have used is considered slang, or colloquial, or perhaps even illiterate, and therefore out of place in the formal style of standard written English that is generally demanded of you. If the particular usage of a word is "standard" (generally acceptable in cultivated speaking and writing), it will not be labeled. But there may be other definitions of the word listed, and these will be labeled in various ways: for example, as *slang, colloq.* (colloquial), *illit.* (illiterate).

GLOSSARY OF COMMON ERRORS IN DICTION

Accept, except. Do not confuse these words. The meaning of *accept* is "to receive" or "to agree to" something: "I accepted his offer." *Except,* used as a verb, can only mean "to exclude": "He was excepted from the list of prize winners."

Ad. In formal English, use the full word *advertisement.*

Affect, effect. Do not confuse these words. As a verb, "to affect" means "to influence": "His speech affected many people." "To effect" means "to bring about," or "to cause": "It is hard to effect a change in society." When you incorrectly use *affect* as a noun, change it to *effect,* which means "result": "The effect of the blow was to split the stone in half."

Aggravate. "Aggravate" means "to make worse." It is not a synonym for "irritate" or "annoy." Do not write: "His snide remarks *aggravated* me." Write: "His snide remarks *irritated* me." Further insults would, of course, *aggravate* your irritated condition.

Allusion, illusion. An *allusion* is an indirect reference, but an *illusion* is a false or deceptive notion.

Among, between. Ordinarily, *between* is used when only two items are spoken of: "I divided the food between the cat and the dog." *Among* relates to more than two items: "The prize money was divided among the three winners."

Amount, number. When things or people can be counted individually, use *number:* "There was a large number of students in the hall." When you are referring to a quantity of something which is not thought of in terms of individual, countable units, use *amount:* "A large amount of gold was discovered in the mountain."

Anyways, anywheres. Use the standard forms, *anyway* and *anywhere.*

Around. Do not use the colloquial "around" in expressions like "He left *around* ten o'clock," or, "I can recite *around* fifteen poems." Use "about": "He left *about* ten o'clock." "I can recite *about* fifteen poems."

As. *As* in the sense of "because" is often not as clear as *because, for,* or *since.* "I would like to leave because (not *as*) I'm tired." See also **Like.**

At. See **Where at.**

Awhile, a while. After a preposition, spell as two words: "I slept for a while." Otherwise spell as one word: "I slept awhile."

Because. See **Reason is because.**

Being as, being that. *Because* or *since* are preferred in Standard English.

Beside, besides. *Beside* means "at the side of"; *besides* means "in addition to." "*Besides* chicken, we ate roast beef and bananas as we sat *beside* the stream."

Bust, busted. These are substandard forms of the verb *burst.* Use *burst* in present and past tenses. *Bursted* does not exist.

Compare to, compare with. *To compare to* means to state that something is *similar to* something else: "He compared the coffee *to* mud." *To compare with* means to investigate the similarities and differences between two things: "He compared the female students *with* the male students and found the females brighter."

Complected.   Substandard for *complexioned.*

Could of.   Illiterate for *could have.*

Data.   This word is a Latin plural (singular, *datum*) and is often used in English with plural verbs and pronouns: *"These* data *are* out of date." Many educated people equally accept its use in the singular: *"This* data *is* no longer useful." (See **Strata, Phenomena.**)

Don't is a contraction of *do not* and must not be confused with *does not* or *doesn't.* ERROR: "He don't mind insults." CORRECTION: **"He *doesn't* (or *does not*) mind insults."**

Effect.   See **Affect.**

Enthuse.   In formal English, it is better to use *to become enthusiastic.*

Equally as good.   Drop the *as* and write "equally good," or use "just as good."

Except.   See **Accept.**

Farther, further.   *Farther* is often preferred to express extent in *space,* whereas *further* is preferred to express extent in *time* or *degree:* "We walked *farther* into the woods"; "He went *further* in condemning him than anyone expected."

Fewer, less.   When referring to separate items that can be counted, use *fewer:* "You make *fewer* mistakes now than when you started." *Less* refers to the degree or amount of something we consider as a whole, and not as a series of individual items: "I have *less* money now than when I started."

Hadn't ought.   Illiterate. Instead of saying, "I hadn't ought to have gone," say, **"I shouldn't have gone."**

Heathful, healthy.   The usual preference is that whatever *gives* health is *healthful* ("a healthful climate") and that whatever *has* health is healthy ("a healthy person").

Illusion. See **Allusion.**

In regards to. Use *in regard to.*

Irregardless. The correct form is *regardless.*

Kind of, sort of. In standard written English, change this expression to *somewhat, rather, a little:* "I was somewhat (not *kind of*) annoyed."

Lay, lie. When you mean "to put," use *lay.* The forms of "to lay" are "I *lay* the book down" (present), "I *laid* the book down" (past), and "I *have laid* the book down" (present perfect). When you mean "to recline," use lie. The forms of "to lie" are "I *lie* in my bed" (present), "I *lay* in my bed" (past), and "I *have lain* in my bed" (present perfect).

Less. See **Fewer.**

Like, as, as if. *Like* is a preposition and is correctly used in phrases *like* this or the following: "He looks *like* my father." It is incorrectly used when followed by a clause. ERROR: "It looks *like* my father enjoys your company." CORRECTION: Change *like* to *as if.* **"It looks as if my father enjoys your company."** In the sentence, "I behaved *like* I was told to," change *like* to *as.* **"I behaved as I was told to."**

May of, might of. Illiterate for *may have, might have.*

Mighty. Use a standard word like *very:* "I was very (not *mighty*) tired."

Most. Use *almost:* "I saw him almost (not *most*) every day."

Must of. Illiterate for *must have.*

Nice. A word expressing a vaguely favorable attitude toward something. Avoid it in formal writing by using a more exact word.

Of. Illiterate for *have* in *could of, might of,* etc.

Off of. Drop the *of.*

Phenomena. In formal English, *phenomena* is the plural, *phenomenon* the singular.

Quite. Do not overuse to mean *very,* as in "quite good," "quite hard," etc.

Real. Keep expressions like "real good," "real exciting," out of your written English. Use "*really* good" or "very good."

Reason is because. ERROR: "The *reason* I told you *is because* I can trust you." CORRECTION 1: Change *because* to *that* ("**The reason I told you is *that* I can trust you**"). CORRECTION 2. Recast the sentence ("**I told you because I can trust you**").

Should of. Illiterate for *should have.*

So. 1. Do not overuse *so* as a conjunction joining main clauses. See **Subordination.**

2. Do not use *so* where you could use *so that:* Change "I came to visit you *so* we could have a chat" to "**I came to visit you *so that* we could have a chat.**"

3. Do not overuse *so* as a "feminine intensive": "I was so disappointed." "She is so nice, isn't she?" Try substituting *very,* or *extremely.*

Sort of. See **Kind of.**

Strata. The singular is *stratum.* Use *strata* only as a plural.

Sure. Use *certainly,* or *surely:* "I surely (not *sure*) was tired."

Try and. Substitute *try to.*

Where at. In a sentence like "I know where he is at," *at* is unnecessary and should be dropped. "**I know where he is.**"

Which, who. Use *who* (or *that*), but never use *which* to refer to persons. "Here is the man who (not *which*) is responsible."

While. This is mainly a conjunction of time: "I ran while I still had time." Do not overwork it to mean *and, but,* or *whereas:* "I loved roses, but (not *while*) she preferred daisies."

Would of. Illiterate for *would have.*

[dict] DICTIONARY

Consult your dictionary for the meaning of this word. (See DICTION.)

[em] [emph] EMPHASIS

1. Rearrange your sentence to give the important words and phrases their proper emphasis. The position of greatest emphasis is the *end* of your sentence. Next in emphasis is the beginning of your sentence.

2. Change the weak *passive* voice of the verb to the strong *active* voice.

1. EMPHASIS THROUGH PROPER WORD ORDER.

Poor emphasis: We jammed into the car and started on our trip *in the morning, just after the sun rose.* (The italicized phrases are the least important elements of the sentence, but are placed at the end, the position of *most* emphasis.)

Proper emphasis: In the morning, just after the sun rose, we jammed into the car and started on our trip. (The main clause, beginning "we jammed," is now properly emphasized.)

2. EMPHASIS THROUGH ACTIVE VOICE.

Unemphatic passive voice: At camp, many games were played by the children which were not played at home.
Emphatic active voice: At camp, the children played many games which they did not play at home.

[fog]   **FOGGY WRITING**

Your writing is entirely unclear. **Rewrite completely, but first think through the ideas again step by step.** (See AWKWARDNESS and COHERENCE.)

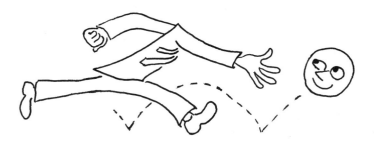

FRAGMENTARY SENTENCES

You have written only a phrase or a subordinate clause, or some other *piece* of a sentence, but not a full sentence. **If you can logically attach what you have written to the previous or the following sentence, do so. If not, then expand your fragment into a full sentence.** A full sentence is able to stand alone as a complete thought.

In the following examples, sentence fragments are in italics:

Error: I do not have the steadiest hand in the world. *As you can see from my writing.*

Correction: (The fragment is a subordinate clause which should be attached to the previous sentence by a comma.) **I do not have the steadiest hand in the world, as you can see from my writing.**

Error: He lectured on many interesting things. *For example, about magic.*

Correction: (The fragment is a phrase. It is better style to make a complete sentence out of it than to add it to the previous sentence.) **He lectured on many interesting things.** *He spoke,* **for example, about magic.**

Error: John would not make a good captain. *A good player, yes, but not always a good sport.*

Correction: (The fragment here is the complement of a subject and verb which were both omitted. Supply them.) John would not make a good captain. *He is* a good player, yes, but not always a good sport.

[inc]   INCOMPLETE CONSTRUCTIONS

Add the word or words necessary to complete the construction you now have. Examples:

Preposition omitted: She was greatly interested and enthusiastic about the project.

Correction: She was greatly interested *in* and enthusiastic about the project.

Verb omitted: The people were all interesting and my vacation, in general, wonderful.

Correction: The people were all interesting and my vacation, in general, *was* wonderful. (The plural verb *were*, used with *people*, cannot agree with the singular noun *vacation*.)

Verb omitted: We never have and never shall attack without provocation.

Correction: We never have *attacked* and never shall attack without provocation. (The auxiliary verb *have* must be followed by *attacked*.)

Incomplete comparison: When I leave school, I may not be more intelligent, but I shall certainly be a well-rounded person.

Correction: When I leave school, I may not be more intelligent *than when I started*, but I shall certainly be a well-rounded person. (The comparative *more* needs a *than*-clause to complete it. See COMPARISONS.)

[ital]	**ITALICS**

Underline the titles of books, magazines, newspapers, plays, and movies. Do not put quotation marks around them.

Underline foreign words and expressions.

Underline words or letters if they are not used for their meaning, but as words or letters only.

Examples: The <u>Atlantic Monthly</u>, The <u>Return of the Native</u>, <u>King Lear</u>; <u>coup d'état</u>, <u>comme il faut</u>, <u>persona non grata</u>; Add a <u>u</u> to <u>gaze</u> and you get <u>gauze</u>.

Note: Underlined words appear, when printed, in italic or slanted type, *like this.*

[mod]	**MISPLACED MODIFIERS**

1. Place the word or phrase marked as misplaced in a closer or clearer relation to the word it modifies.

2. Do not awkwardly split infinitives.

1. MISPLACED MODIFIERS.

Error: I *only* know one thing.

Correction: I know *only* one thing.

Error: The emperor was just and kind to people *in his way.*

Correction: (The student's error makes it seem as if the emperor were kind to his enemies!) *In his way,* the emperor was just and kind to people.

Error: He fell while he was running *into a manhole.*

Correction: He fell *into a manhole* while he was running.

Error: The man who was working *quickly* swallowed his lunch.

Correction: This is a case of a "squinting" modifier. Does *quickly* modify *working* or *swallowed?* If it modifies *swallowed,* then write: **The man who was working swallowed his lunch** *quickly.*

2. SPLIT INFINITIVE.

Error: The cat began *to* industriously *lick* its paws.

Correction: (Do not needlessly separate the two halves of an infinitive by wedging an adverb between them.) **The cat began** *to lick* **its paws industriously.**

[mx]   MIXED CONSTRUCTIONS

You began your sentence with one construction or figure of speech, then shifted to another which cannot logically or grammatically complete the sentence. **Change one part of the sentence so that it harmonizes with the rest.** Examples:

Mixed sentence parts: Learning to love the beauty of nature, the endless variety of things around you, the air itself, and you will be a complete person.

Correction: Change *learning* to *learn.* **Learn to love the beauty of nature, the endless variety of things around you, the air itself, and you will be a complete person.**

Mixed sentence parts: By throwing the upper right-hand lever is the way to stop the machine.

Correction: Drop the first word, *by.* **Throwing the upper right-hand lever is the way to stop the machine.** (If the writer wants to keep the beginning of his sentence, he will have to change the end: **By throwing the upper right-hand lever *one stops* the machine.**)

Mixed sentence parts: I bought a picture which, in hanging it upside down, made no difference in the effect it made.

Correction: (The main grammatical confusion lies in the *which* clause, "which . . . made no difference in the effect it made." The pronoun *which* stands for the noun *picture,* and so the clause illogically says, "the *picture* made no difference in the effect it made.") **I bought a picture which could be hung upside down without any difference in the effect it made.**

Mixed metaphors: The wheels of fate moved their grimy *hands.* (Since when do wheels have hands? As you can see, mixing figures of speech can result in an absurd, illogical image—funny, but not intentionally so.)

Mixed metaphors: A tongue of land jutted out from the foot of the cliff. (It is absurd to imagine a foot sticking out its tongue.)

[No cap]   NO CAPITALIZATION

Do not capitalize the word or words indicated. (See CAPITALIZATION.)

[No ¶]   NO PARAGRAPH

Do not begin a new paragraph at this point. (See PARAGRAPHING.)

[No Pn]   NO PUNCTUATION

Do not insert any punctuation at this point. (See PUNCTUATION.)

[num]   NUMBERS

Spell out any figures that can be spoken in one or two words. Use numerals for any sum that must be expressed in three or more words.

Examples: thirty, fifty-five, 172.

PARAGRAPHING

Begin a new paragraph at the place marked.

In formal essay writing, no paragraph should consist of less than two sentences. One sentence, usually the first, is the "topic" sentence and states the general idea of the paragraph. The other sentences should stick to the "topic" and develop the main idea through details, or examples, or logical argument.

Each sentence should flow from the previous sentence and lead to the following one in a clear and logical manner (see COHERENCE.) Here is a paragraph written by a student in which the first sentence states the "topic" and the following sentences *develop* the topic through illustrative detail:

> You will see only the hardiest citizens among us greeting the cold weather with a welcoming smile. If you watch through an unfrosted corner of your window, you will see them striding briskly along, rosy-cheeked, and breathing in deeply the chill air. No gloves cover their ruddy knuckles, no scarves wrap their necks, and no ear-muffs stifle the angry whistling of the wind that to their ears is as sweet as birdsong. They walk along in light jackets, their shirts open at the neck, as if this were as balmy a day as any in the year.

PARALLELISM

Keep sentence elements of equal importance in parallel form.

Notice the method of correcting the errors below:

Error: I enjoy going to movies, listening to music, and cards.

Correction: I enjoy going to movies, listening to music, and *playing* cards. (A parallel *-ing* word is needed before cards.)

Error: She learned to type up reports, to file correspondence, and how to smile pleasantly.

Correction: She learned to type up reports, to file correspondence, and *to smile* pleasantly. (The "how" upsets the pattern of three parallel infinitives.)

Error: The opinion of one off-beat columnist is that the mayor is adept at underhand dealings profitable only to himself, and we should therefore throw him out of office.

Correction: The opinion of one off-beat columnist is that the mayor is adept at underhand dealings profitable only to himself, and *that* we should therefore throw him out of office. (The second "that" makes it clear that the opinion which follows is solely the columnist's and does not belong to the writer of the sentence. You can see how important clear parallelism can be!)

Error: He always plays the piano with ease, with confidence, and takes pleasure in it.

Correction: He always plays **the piano with ease, with confidence, and** *with pleasure.* (We now have a series of parallel prepositional phrases.)

[pass]   PASSIVE VOICE

Change the verb from the passive voice to the active voice in order to gain directness. (See EMPHASIS.)

Weak passive voice: With the changing of seasons there comes a change in the type of clothing *to be worn.*

Direct active voice: With the changing of seasons there comes a change in the type of clothing *people wear.*

Passive: In the fall, cotton clothes *are stored away* by families and all that *can be seen* is bulky woolens.

Active: In the fall, *families store away* their cotton clothes and all·*one can see* is bulky woolens.

Passive: I am sure this *can be done* by us if the money *can be found.*

Active: I am sure *we can do* this if *we can find* the money.

PUNCTUATION

Insert the correct punctuation.

In most cases, students either fail to use commas when needed or else they use them too often. If you study the few simple directions given below under the section for COMMAS, most of your punctuation troubles will be over.

Note: The marks of punctuation are discussed below in alphabetical order.

[ap]
[apos]

APOSTROPHE [']

Add a missing apostrophe, or remove one you have mistakenly used.

The apostrophe has two main uses: 1. It marks the possessive case of nouns. 2. It indicates a contraction.

1. FORMING THE POSSESSIVE CASE OF NOUNS.

a. For nouns, both singular and plural, that do not end in *s*, form the possessive by adding ['s]: the **bird's** nest; the **children's** party; the **person's** name.

b. For plural nouns that end in *s,* add the apostrophe only: the **soldiers'** uniforms (uniforms of the soldiers); **ladies'** coats (coats for ladies).

c. For singular nouns that end in *s,* add [*'s*]. But if the last *s* would be awkward to pronounce, then drop it and add only the apostrophe: the **boss's** daughter (daughter of the boss), *but* **Rameses'** kingdom, **Moses'** leadership.

2. THE APOSTROPHE IN CONTRACTIONS.

Always use the apostrophe to show the omission of a letter or letters in the contracted form of words:

Wasn't (was not), **I've** (I have), **we'll** (we will), **you're** (you are), **it's** (it is).

COLON [:]

Place the colon after an introductory statement to call attention to what follows, such as an explanation, a list of items, or a long quotation. See the following examples:

1. COLON INTRODUCING AN EXPLANATION.

Here is my honest opinion: I think you are a crackpot. (When a full sentence follows a colon, you may capitalize the first word or not, as you please. If a *quoted* sentence follows the colon, you *must* begin the sentence with a capital letter. EXAMPLE: The sign was all too clear: "No swimming in this area.")

2. COLON BEFORE A LIST OF ITEMS.

Be sure to take the following things with you on a long ocean voyage: plenty of books, a deck of cards, a chess set, and a warm blanket.

3. COLON BEFORE A LONG QUOTATION.

In "An Apology for Idlers," Robert Louis Stevenson says: "There is a sort of dead-alive, hackneyed people about, who are scarcely conscious of living except in the exercise of some conventional occupation. Bring these fellows into the country, or set them aboard ship, and you will see how they pine for their desk or their study."

[C]   **COMMA [,]**

The following five directions for using the comma will solve practically all the comma problems you will ever have.

1. Use the comma before coordinating conjunctions (*and, but, or, nor, for*) that join two main clauses.

Examples:

I completely forgot about our date for last night, *and* I sincerely hope that you will try to understand.

Stop going with other girls behind my back, *or* I promise I'll never see you again.

Exception: If the main clauses are very short, you do not have to separate them with a comma. As an example, take the boy's obvious reply to the girl's ultimatum:

I never have *and* I never will.

2. Use the comma after sentence elements that appear before the main clause, such as subordinate clauses and phrases.

Examples:

When he spoke to the student, the instructor asked him whether he studied very much.

Shaking his head, the student replied that his brothers kept the TV blaring day and night.

As a solution to the problem, the instructor recommended the temporary removal of a few tubes from the set.

Exception: Most very short prepositional phrases that come before a main clause are not followed by a comma:

After a moment the student admitted that TV wasn't his only distraction from studying.

But certain introductory words and phrases, like *for example, in short, in fact, however, consequently,* are used to form a bridge, or transition, from one sentence to another, and are always followed by a comma:

In conclusion, we all had a merry time.

(See TRANSITIONS.)

3. Use commas to set off parenthetical sentence elements.

A sentence element is parenthetical, or *nonrestrictive,* if it supplies information not essential to the clear meaning of the sentence.

In the following examples, the nonrestrictive elements are italicized.

Examples:

Modern automobiles, *which at last have gotten rid of their tail fins,* strike me as more attractive than the older models.

He is, *I am sure,* a good sport.

They are gone, *thank goodness.*

Test for parenthetical elements: To test whether an element is parenthetical, remove it from the sentence.

If the basic idea of the sentence remains the same, and is not distorted, then the element you have removed is parenthetical and should be set off by commas. Read the above examples without the words in italics, and you will find that the ideas of the original sentences remain unchanged.

Restrictive elements: Restrictive sentence elements are necessary to the meaning of the sentence, as in this example:

All men *who are hard of hearing* should wear hearing aids.

Notice that the clause "who are hard of hearing" is *essential* to the meaning of the sentence. If you remove it, the basic idea of the sentence is distorted. Restrictive elements, as you can see, are not set apart from the rest of the sentence by commas.

4. Use commas between items in a series.

A series consists of three or more elements, which may be single *words, phrases,* or *clauses* (these last three italicized words are in a series).

Examples:

The basement was *dark, damp,* and *cold.* (The formula for the series is *a, b,* and *c.*)

He stumbled *down the stairs, across the room,* and *through the doorway.* (A series of three prepositional phrases.)

I asked them *when I could come, where I could stay,* and *what I could do.* (A series of three subordinate clauses.)

I whistled shrilly, I listened in vain, and I turned sadly away. (Three main clauses, if they are very short, may be connected in a series by commas.)

5. Use commas between coordinate adjectives that come before a noun.

Examples:

> She is an *old, faithful* servant.
> Look at his *clear, twinkling* eyes.

The test for coordinate adjectives is to insert the word *and* between them and omit the comma. If the adjectives are coordinate (equal in rank), you will feel no awkwardness in reading them: *clear and twinkling* eyes.

The test shows that the following examples are not coordinate adjectives: a *small living* room, a *little old* man. The last adjective in each pair is really treated as part of the noun. It would be awkward to say "a small and living room," or "a little and old man." Where you can insert the *and,* use the comma. Where you cannot insert the *and,* omit the comma.

DASH [—]

For the most part, avoid using the dash if commas or parentheses will serve equally well. Use the dash to mark an abrupt shift in thought, or to set off a parenthetical element that you wish to make emphatic.

Examples:

> "I would like—no, as a matter of fact, I wouldn't." (Abrupt shift in thought.)
>
> I must admit—since you force me to tell you—that my opinion of you is not very high. (Dashes set off a parenthetical element emphatically. Parentheses seem to muffle and make unemphatic the material they enclose.)

ELLIPSIS [. . .]

In formal writing, the ellipsis—three double-spaced periods—is used only to show that you have omitted material from a quoted passage.

Example:

"Poetry turns all things to loveliness; it exalts the beauty of that which is most beautiful, and it adds beauty to that which is most deformed; . . . it subdues to union . . . all irreconcilable things."

—Percy Bysshe Shelley

EXCLAMATION POINT [!]

The exclamation point is used to express *strong* feeling. Do not overuse it.

Examples:

What a wonderful, wonderful day! (Exuberance.)
Get out of here! (A brisk command.)

PARENTHESES [( )]

Use parentheses to enclose material that is clearly supplementary and not essential to the meaning of the sentence. Whatever is enclosed in parentheses appears unimportant to the reader. Use parentheses very sparingly; never use them when you can use commas instead.

Examples of the correct use of parentheses:

I walked right up to him (no one was with him at the time) and told him what we had decided.

Last week he came up with a brilliant new idea (the seeds of it had been ripening in his mind for months) only to see it rejected as absurd by the committee.

Incorrect use of parentheses:

His brother told him (John) not to annoy him (Allen) anymore. (You cannot compensate for poor reference of pronouns by using explanatory parentheses. The sentence would have to be rewritten for smoothness of style *and* clear meaning as well.)

Error: The material she bought was aqua (not blue) and didn't match her dress.

Correction: (Do not use parentheses where you can use commas.) **The material she bought was aqua, not blue, and didn't match her dress.**

[quot]   QUOTATION MARKS [" "]

Use a pair of quotation marks (" ") 1. to enclose a passage of directly quoted words; 2. to draw attention to an unusual word; and 3. to set off the titles of chapters, articles, stories, and poems published as *part* of a complete book or magazine.

When using other punctuation marks at the end of a quoted passage, always keep the period and comma *before* the end quotation mark. Always put semicolons and colons *after* the end quotation mark.

1. DIRECTLY QUOTED PASSAGES.

Examples:

> The stewardess said, "Fasten your seat belts, please."
> Alexander Pope says that hope "springs eternal in the human breast."

Do not use quotation marks for indirect quotations:

Error: My brother said "that he was unhappy about the outcome."

Correction: Remove the quotation marks. **My brother said that he was unhappy about the outcome.** (Quotation marks would be used if this sentence were changed to a direct quotation, as follows: My brother said, "I am unhappy about the outcome.")

> Quotations broken by "he said," "she said," etc.:

> "I suppose," he remarked, "that success comes only with time." (Since the quoted passage is one complete sentence, the interrupting words are set off by commas and *not* followed by a period or semicolon.)
> "I understand the plan," Jim said. "I think it might work." (In this case, two separate sentences are quoted. *Jim said* must be followed by a period, for it marks the end of one quoted sentence.)

2. EMPHASIS OF UNUSUAL WORDS.

Examples:

> In the printing trade, an engraved plate is called a "cut."
> The jazz musician I met said he "dug" me and enjoyed spending the evening at my "pad."

3. STORIES, ARTICLES, AND OTHER PARTS OF A BOOK OR MAGAZINE.

Examples:

> One of my favorite stories is Hemingway's "The Killers."
> When you read *Sister Carrie,* pay careful attention to

the first chapter, "The Magnet Attracting: A Waif Amid Forces." (Note that the title of the whole book is underlined, or italicized, whereas the chapter title is in quotation marks.)

QUOTATION MARKS WITH OTHER PUNCTUATION:

1. Periods and commas are placed *inside* closing quotation marks:

> Shakespeare said, "Unquiet meals make ill digestions."
> Francis Bacon remarked that "the monuments of wit survive the monuments of power," and I wholly agree with him.

2. Colons and semicolons are placed *outside* closing quotation marks:

> We had arrived at "the moment of truth": the matador extended his sword for the finishing stroke.
> I know that "to err is human"; yet fifteen errors in one ball game is too much to forgive.

3. Question marks and exclamation points remain inside closing quotation marks *only* if they are a part of the quoted passage, as in the first two examples below. Otherwise, such marks remain outside the quotation marks, as in the last two examples:

> I asked her, "Is dinner ready?"
> He shouted, "Advance or I'll fire!"
> Did I just hear you say, "Dinner is ready"?
> Stop saying "yes"!

In direct quotations, avoid the extra comma or period after a closing quotation mark:

Error: "Well, well!", he said.
Correction: (Remove comma.) **"Well, well!" he said.**

Error: He asked, "What's your name?".
Correction: (Remove the period.) **He asked, "What's your name?"**

4. Use single marks (' ') to set off a quotation within a quotation:

"When Caesar said 'I came, I saw, I conquered,'" my history teacher declared, "little did he know that he had invented the telegram."

[semi] SEMICOLON [;]

1. Use the semicolon to separate sentence elements equal in rank when they contain commas.

2. Use the semicolon to separate two main clauses when they are closely related in idea but are *not* connected with a coordinating conjunction (*and, but, for, or, nor*).

1. EQUAL SENTENCE ELEMENTS CONTAINING COMMAS.

I introduced him to Jack Kreel, the president; Will Baum, the vice-president; Herb Dunn, the treasurer; and Frank Newhouse, the secretary.

2. MAIN CLAUSES NOT CONNECTED BY A CONJUNCTION.

It is not so much the threatening weather that concerns me; it is the dilapidated condition of the ship. (The ideas are closely related.)

Also use the semicolon between main clauses connected by certain conjunctive adverbs, like *however* and *therefore* (see COMMA SPLICE):

I would like to attend the conference; however, I have a prior appointment which I am unable to cancel.

Do not use the semicolon between a main clause and a phrase or subordinate clause:

Error: I do not like to eat orange peels; although I admit that in marmalade they are quite good.

Correction: Change the semicolon to a comma. **I do not like to eat orange peels, although I admit that in marmalade they are quite good.**

Error: The fire spread through the town in a matter of minutes; lighting up the sky with a devilish glare.

Correction: Change the semicolon to a comma. **The fire spread through the town in a matter of minutes, lighting up the sky with a devilish glare.**

[ref] REFERENCE OF PRONOUNS

Make the pronoun you have used clearly refer to a previous noun.

Error: When John spoke to Peter, he said he didn't think *he*'d be invited to the party. (Does the last *he* refer to John or Peter?)

Correction: When John spoke to Peter, he said, "I don't think I (or *you*) will be invited to the party." (The use of direct quotation often solves these reference problems.)

Error: She felt as if she would burst into tears, *which* made it difficult for her to speak. (The pronoun *which* is often incorrectly used, as it is here, to refer to the whole preceding main clause rather than to a single noun.)

Correction: She felt as if she would burst into tears, a *sensation which* made it difficult for her to speak. (Place a noun before *which* that sums up the whole idea referred to. When this method seems too awkward, try recasting a part or the whole of the sentence: *Feeling* as if she would burst into tears, *she found it difficult to speak.*)

Error: Daily she scrubbed the floors, mended his clothes, cooked him three hearty meals fit for a king, and spoke only of things that would please him. *This* proved her utter devotion to him. (The pronoun *this* is awkwardly made to refer to the whole preceding sentence.)

Correction (of the second sentence): Combine the pronoun *this* with a noun, or perhaps an adjective-noun group, which sums up the ideas of the whole previous sentence. **This** *ceaseless slavery* **proved her utter devotion to him.**

Error: How can one not be happy when he sees the leaves return in the spring and the difference *it* makes in everything about him? (The pronoun *it* awkwardly refers to the whole previous clause, "the leaves return in the spring.")

Correction: **How can one not be happy when he sees** *the return of the leaves* **in the spring and the difference it makes in everything about him?** (Now *it* clearly refers to the noun *return.*)

<hr>

[R] [rep]　REPETITION

Do not awkwardly repeat the same word or idea you have used before. (See also WORDINESS.)

Error: A cool breeze was *blowing,* and the brownish gold leaves were being *blown* about by the wind.

Correction: Change *blown* to *swept,* or find some other good synonym. Sometimes, as in this case, the sentence would be better if it were condensed: **The brownish gold leaves were being swept about by the cool breeze.** (There is no need to refer to the breeze again, even by the synonym *wind.*)

Error: The air was too cold, *and* while I was asleep it chilled me, *and* when I awoke my bones felt stiff.

Correction: Eliminate one of the *and*'s: **The air was too cold. While I was asleep it chilled me, and when I awoke my bones felt stiff.**

Error: The steam could be seen rising from the radiator. *The steam* turned to frost on the windowpane.

Correction: Change the second *steam* to the pronoun *it*. **The steam could be seen rising from the radiator. It turned to frost on the windowpane.**

Error: He *walked up and down* and kept pacing about the room.

Correction: Avoid repeating the same idea. **He kept pacing about the room.**

RUN-ON SENTENCE

Be careful not to run one sentence into the next with no punctuation separating them. **End the first sentence with a period, and begin the next with a capital letter.** (Do not join two sentences with a comma, either. This error, sometimes called a run-on sentence, is more usually referred to as a *comma splice*. See COMMA SPLICE.)

Error: He enjoys watching them play ball he thinks they're great.

Correction: **He enjoys watching them play ball. He thinks they're great.**

Error: She put on her bathing cap then she plunged into the water.

Correction: **She put on her bathing cap. Then she plunged into the water.** (Although a period is correct, a semicolon would probably be better between *cap* and *then*. Look up the use of semicolons before conjunctive adverbs like *then*, *however*, and *therefore* under COMMA SPLICE.)

[SS] SENTENCE STRUCTURE

You have made an obvious error in the structure of your sentence. If no more specific directions are given for correcting it, read it over carefully, sounding it aloud if you can. You can often hear an error that you cannot see. If you still cannot locate the trouble, you would do best to **rewrite the sentence** entirely. (See COHERENCE.)

SHIFT IN POINT OF VIEW

If they are not logically necessary, avoid shifts in 1. person—from *I* or *one* to *you*; 2. subject and voice; 3. tense; 4. mood.

1. SHIFTS IN PERSON.

Error: If one stops to watch them work, *you* are greeted with a smile.

Correction: If one stops to watch them work, *one* is greeted with a smile.

Error: This was a morning that made me button up my jacket and made *you* wish *you* had worn a topcoat.

Correction: This was a morning that made me button up my jacket and wish *I* had worn a topcoat. (No need to repeat "made me.")

2. SHIFTS IN SUBJECT AND VOICE.

Error: *A party was attended by us* after we graduated. (Notice the awkward passive voice of the verb that makes *party* the subject.)

Correction: *We attended a party* **after we graduated.** (Now the subject of both clauses is the same, *we*, and both verbs are in the *active* voice. See PASSIVE VOICE.)

3. SHIFTS IN TENSE.

Error: He rushed to catch his train but *misses* it by half a minute. (Needless shift from past to present tense.)

Correction: **He rushed to catch his train but** *missed* **it by half a minute.**

4. SHIFTS IN MOOD.

The only shifts in mood likely to occur as an error in your writing are shifts from the *command* (imperative) form of the verb to the ordinary *indicative* form of the verb, as in the following example:

Error: Be sure to visit the science exhibition, and then *you must go* to the art show.

Correction: **Be sure to visit the science exhibition, and then** *go* **to the art show.** (Both verbs, "be" and "go," are now in the command form.)

[sub]   SUBORDINATION

When ideas are *not* of equal importance, do not arrange them in a series of short, choppy sentences or in a series of main clauses connected by *and*'s, *but*'s, and *so*'s.

Give emphasis to the more important ideas by keeping them as main clauses. Change lesser ideas into subordinate clauses, phrases, and even single words where possible.

Examples:

Poor: Her employer did not care for her, *so* he refused to write her a letter of recommendation. (Two equally emphatic main clauses.)

Better: *Because* her employer did not care for her, he refused to write her a letter of recommendation. (The first main clause, less emphatic than the second, is changed into a subordinate clause beginning with *because*.)

Poor: He was exhausted. He had been swimming too long and was doubled up by a sudden cramp. He called for help. (This is an awkward series of choppy sentences.)

Better: Exhausted from swimming too long and doubled up by a sudden cramp, he called for help. (The first two sentences are turned into phrases.)

Poor: The moon was glowing and it looked like the face of a snowman.

Better: The *glowing* moon looked like the face of a snowman. (The first main clause is condensed into the single word *glowing*.)

[T]   TENSE

1. One of the verbs of your sentence may not be in the correct time relation with the other(s). Check to see whether you are using the proper sequence of tenses.

2. Use your dictionary to find the correct forms of "irregular" verbs (for example, *choose, chose, chosen*).

3. Do not shift tenses without good reason. (See *Shifts in Tense* under SHIFT IN POINT OF VIEW.)

1. SEQUENCE OF TENSES.

If the time when an action takes place is the *same* in both the main clause and the subordinate clause, then the tense of both verbs must be the same.

Examples:

When he *arrived,* the crowd *greeted* him with a long ovation.

As he slowly *turns,* he *balances* himself with his arms.

If the action in the subordinate clause is earlier than that in the main clause, put the subordinate verb in the appropriate past tense.

Examples:

I *am* informed that he *has worked* wonders. (Main verb, *am*, is in present tense; subordinate verb, *has worked*, is in present perfect tense. The present perfect expresses a time earlier than the present.)

I *was* informed that he *had worked* wonders. (The past perfect, *had worked*, expresses a time prior to some understood time in the past. This "understood" past time is expressed by the simple past tense, *was*.)

When you are expressing *a permanent fact*, however, the present tense is used:

I was informed that penicillin *works* wonders. (Use *works*, not *worked*.)

Keep an infinitive in the present tense if it expresses the same time as the action of the main verb; keep it in the past tense if it expresses a time before the action of the main verb.

Examples:

I would have liked *to go* with you.

I would like *to go* with you. (In both these cases, although the main verb differs in tense, the present infinitive concerns "going" at the same time that the "liking," or desire to go, is expressed.)

I would like *to have gone* with you. (Here the past infinitive is used because the wish in the present concerns an action already completed in the past.)

Error: I would *have liked* to *have gone* with you. (Do not use the past infinitive together with the past tense of the main verb. Use one or the other, as shown in the examples above, but not both at the same time.)

2. IRREGULAR VERBS.

Most English verbs are "regular," forming their past tense and past participle in *-ed*: I *waited*, I have *waited*.

Once you know the present tense, *wait*, you know all the other tenses. There is a troublesome group of "irregular" verbs, however, whose present tense (I *break*) is no clue to the past tense (I *broke*) or to the compound past tenses formed with the past participle (I have *broken: broken* is the past participle).

If you are in doubt about the past tense forms of a verb, look up the verb in the dictionary under its present tense form (*bite*, for example) and you will find the past tense (*bit*) and past participle (*bitten*) listed in order right after it. Below is a list of some of the most frequently misused irregular verbs:

PRESENT	PAST	PAST PARTICIPLE
I *blow*	I *blew*	I have *blown*
I *bring*	I *brought*	I have *brought*
I *burst*	I *burst*	I have *burst*
I *do*	I *did*	I have *done*
I *drink*	I *drank*	I have *drunk*
I *eat*	I *ate*	I have *eaten*
I *forbid*	I *forbade*	I have *forbidden*
I *go*	I *went*	I have *gone*
I *lay* (bricks)	I *laid* (bricks)	I have *laid* (bricks)
I *lie* (down)	I *lay* (down)	I have *lain* (down)
I *ring*	I *rang*	I have *rung*
I *rise*	I *rose*	I have *risen*
I *run*	I *ran*	I have *run*
I *seek*	I *sought*	I have *sought*
I *sing*	I *sang*	I have *sung*
I *steal*	I *stole*	I have *stolen*
I *swim*	I *swam*	I have *swum*
I *swing*	I *swung*	I have *swung*
I *write*	I *wrote*	I have *written*

3. TENSE SHIFTS.

Changes in tense must occur for a good reason. In the following example, there is no reason for the shift:

Error: I ran to his house and tried to find him, but I *arrive* too late.

Correction: Change *arrive* to *arrived*. **I ran to his house and tried to find him, but I *arrived* too late.**

TRANSITIONS

Add a word or phrase to form a logical bridge, or *transition*, between the two thoughts. Without such a connecting element, the second thought does not follow smoothly or logically from the first. (See also COHERENCE.)

Examples:

Transition missing: I liked him. I thought his table manners needed improving. (The sudden contrast between these two thoughts is not smoothly bridged over.)

Better: I liked him. *However,* I thought his table manners needed improving.

Transition missing: On the whole, I think that educated men have made the best politicians. There are exceptions. (The second sentence follows too abruptly.)

Better: On the whole, I think that educated men have made the best politicians. *Of course,* there are exceptions.

Note the use of transitional words and phrases (italicized) in the following—somewhat shortened—paragraph by Schopenhauer:

> What the address is to a letter, the title should be to a book; *in other words,* its main object should be to bring the book to those amongst the public who will take an interest in its contents. It should, *therefore,* be expressive. . . . The worst titles of all are those which have been stolen, *those, I mean,* which have already been borne by other books; for they are *in the first place* a plagiarism, and *secondly* the most convincing proof of a total lack of originality in the author. . . .

TRANSPOSE

Change the order of the indicated words to gain a clearer or more idiomatic reading. (See MISPLACED MODIFIERS.)

Examples:

Poor word order: She raked the *yellow, old* leaves into a pile.

Better: She raked the *old yellow* leaves into a pile. (More natural word order is restored. For the omission of the comma, see page 39 on "coordinate adjectives.")

Poor: I *only* hear good things about him. (*Only* is misplaced.)

Better: I hear *only* good things about him. (*Only* modifies *good* and should be placed next to it.)

[trite] # TRITENESS

Avoid trite expressions, or "clichés"—expressions which are so commonly used that they have lost the original flavor and vividness they once possessed. The overuse of trite expressions implies lazy, unoriginal thinking.

Examples of trite expressions (italicized):

He wanted to live out in *the wide open spaces.*
We made progress *by leaps and bounds.*
On picnics one can relax and enjoy *Mother Nature.*
I felt *as cool as a cucumber.*
We went through many *trials and tribulations.*
Her cousin is *as quiet as a mouse.*

[var] VARIETY IN SENTENCE PATTERNS

To avoid a "choppy" style, **use a variety of sentence types.** For interesting sentence sequences, alternate *simple* with *compound, complex,* and *compound-complex* sentences. If you employ this easy technique, your style—and your grade, too—will improve considerably.

SIMPLE SENTENCE. A simple sentence contains only one main clause. (The sentence you have just read is a simple sentence.) A series of simple sentences in a row can result in choppiness.

Example: I enjoy going to the movies. I like watching murder mysteries best. I sit at the edge of my seat at the high points of such pictures. (None of these sentences is individually bad. But together they are monotonous. Each sentence begins unoriginally in the same way: the pattern is constantly *subject,* then *verb.* See SUBORDINATION after you learn the other sentence types below.)

COMPOUND SENTENCE. A compound sentence consists of two or more simple sentences, or main clauses, usually connected by a coordinating conjunction, like *and, but, or, nor,* or *for.*

Example: Mary still works as a secretary, *but* Harriet has already become a dress designer.

COMPLEX SENTENCE. A complex sentence contains one main clause and one or more subordinate clauses.

Example: Although I sat at the edge of my seat, I did not forget that it was only a movie, after all. (There are two subordinate clauses in this sentence, one beginning with *although,* the other with *that.*)

COMPOUND-COMPLEX SENTENCE. A compound-complex sentence contains at least *two* main clauses and at least *one* subordinate clause.

Example: When we are studying, we should not let outside influences distract us, for our school work deserves our utmost concentration. (The sentence contains one subordinate clause, beginning with *when,* and two main clauses, one beginning with *we* and the other with *for.*)

[wdy]   **WORDINESS**

Express your ideas in fewer words. Do not "puff out" your sentences with unnecessary, repetitious phrasing.

Examples:

Wordy: In my opinion, I personally feel that our system of government is best. ("In my opinion," "personally," and "I feel" are three ways of saying about the same thing. Don't use them all at once!)

Better: I feel that our system of government is best.

Wordy: In the modern world of today, mankind is enjoying the fruits of a long technological revolution which took place throughout the entire period of the machine age.

Better: Today mankind is enjoying the fruits of a long technological revolution. (All that has been left out is mere repetition and adds nothing. See REPETITION.)

You will find the columns below useful for recording the errors you have made in your written assignments throughout the term. Use the first column to list the errors in your first composition, the second column for the errors in your second assignment, etc. For convenience, use the correction symbols only, and next to each write how many times that particular error occurs in that composition: for example, FRAG (2). Record major errors first, then minor. Hopefully, you should see your progress—and your main problems—revealed more and more as the term goes on.

English _____.

ASGT. DATE GRADE	# DATE GRADE	# DATE GRADE	# DATE GRADE	# DATE GRADE	# DATE GRADE	# DATE GRADE	# DATE GRADE	# DATE GRADE	# DATE GRADE	# DATE GRADE

List in the columns below the *correct* forms for the words you misspell on each composition. Your chart will develop into an excellent diagnosis of your spelling problem.

English ———

ASGT. # DATE GRADE	ASGT. # DATE GRADE	ASGT. # DATE GRADE	ASGT. # DATE GRADE	ASGT. # DATE GRADE	ASGT. # DATE GRADE

SPELLING PROGRESS CHART

List in the columns below the *correct* forms for the words you misspell on each composition. Your chart will develop into an excellent diagnosis of your spelling problem.

English ———.

ASGT. # DATE GRADE	ASGT. # DATE GRADE	ASGT. # DATE GRADE	ASGT. # DATE GRADE	ASGT. # DATE GRADE	ASGT. # DATE GRADE

You will find the columns below useful for recording the errors you have made in your written assignments throughout the term. Use the first column to list the errors in your first composition, the second column for the errors in your second assignment, etc. For convenience, use the correction symbols only, and next to each write how many times that particular error occurs in that composition: for example, FRAG (2). Record major errors first, then minor. Hopefully, you should see your progress—and your main problems—revealed more and more as the term goes on.

English ————.

ASGT. DATE GRADE	# DATE GRADE	# DATE GRADE	# DATE GRADE	# DATE GRADE	# DATE GRADE	# DATE GRADE	# DATE GRADE	# DATE GRADE	# DATE GRADE	# DATE GRADE

List in the columns below the *correct* forms for the words you misspell on each composition. Your chart will develop into an excellent diagnosis of your spelling problem.

English ——— .

ASGT. # DATE GRADE	ASGT. # DATE GRADE	ASGT. # DATE GRADE	ASGT. # DATE GRADE	ASGT. # DATE GRADE	ASGT. # DATE GRADE

SPELLING PROGRESS CHART

List in the columns below the *correct* forms for the words you misspell on each composition. Your chart will develop into an excellent diagnosis of your spelling problem.

English ————.

ASGT. # DATE GRADE	ASGT. # DATE GRADE	ASGT. # DATE GRADE	ASGT. # DATE GRADE	ASGT. # DATE GRADE	ASGT. # DATE GRADE